Profiles in Greek and Roman Mythology

ZEUS

P.O. Box 196
Hockessin, Delaware 19707
Visit us on the web: www.mitchelllane.com
Comments? email us: mitchelllane@mitchelllane.com

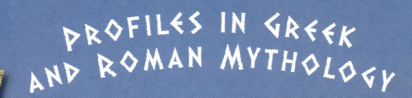

PROFILES IN GREEK AND ROMAN MYTHOLOGY

Titles in the Series

Achilles
Apollo
Artemis
Athena
Dionysus
Hercules
Jason
Odysseus
Perseus
Poseidon
Theseus
Zeus

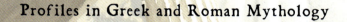

ZEUS

Russell Roberts

Mitchell Lane
PUBLISHERS

P.O. Box 196
Hockessin, Delaware 19707
Visit us on the web: www.mitchelllane.com
Comments? email us: mitchelllane@mitchelllane.com

Copyright © 2008 by Mitchell Lane Publishers. All rights reserved. No part of this book may be reproduced without written permission from the publisher. Printed and bound in the United States of America.

Printing   2   3   4   5   6   7   8   9

Library of Congress Cataloging-in-Publication Data

    Roberts, Russell, 1953-
      Zeus / by Russell Roberts.
        p. cm.—(Profiles in Greek and Roman mythology)
      Includes bibliographical references and index.
      ISBN 978-1-58415-559-1 (library bound)
      1. Zeus (Greek deity)—Juvenile literature. I. Title.
    BL820.J8R63 2007
    398.20938'02—dc22
                                                                                 2007000776

ABOUT THE AUTHOR: Russell Roberts has written nearly 40 books for adults and children on a variety of subjects, including baseball, memory power, business, New Jersey history, and travel. He has written numerous books for Mitchell Lane Publishers, including *Nathaniel Hawthorne, Thomas Jefferson, Holidays and Celebrations in Colonial America, Daniel Boone,* and *The Lost Continent of Atlantis*. He lives in Bordentown, New Jersey, with his family and a fat, fuzzy, and crafty calico cat named Rusti. The mythological Zeus has always interested him. So wise and powerful one moment, yet so amorous and boyish the next, Zeus is a fascinating study in opposites.

MAP CREDIT: p. 15 — Jonathan Scott.

AUTHOR'S NOTE: This story is based on the author's extensive research, which he believes to be accurate. Documentation of such research is contained on page 46. The internet sites referenced herein were active as of the publication date. Due to the fleeting nature of some web sites, we cannot guarantee they will all be active when you are reading this book.
    To reflect current usage, we have chosen to use the secular era designations BCE ("before the common era") and CE ("of the common era") instead of the traditional designations BC ("before Christ") and AD (anno Domini, "in the year of the Lord").

                                                                                                                       PLB / PLB2,4

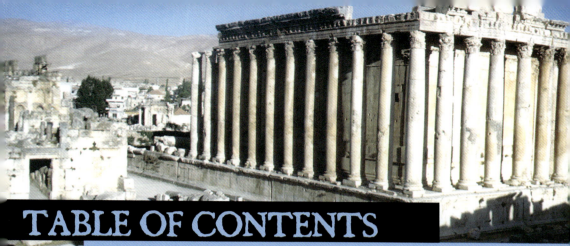

TABLE OF CONTENTS

Profiles in Greek and Roman Mythology

Chapter One
The Birth of Zeus 7
For Your Information: The Titans 13

Chapter Two
The Greek World 15
For Your Information: Cleisthenes 21

Chapter Three
On Mount Olympus 23
For Your Information: Demeter, Persephone, and Hades .. 27

Chapter Four
The Amorous Adventures of Zeus 29
For Your Information: Hercules 35

Chapter Five
Major Zeus Myths 37
For Your Information: Mary Wollstonecraft Shelley 44

Chapter Notes 45
Further Reading 46
    For Young Adults 46
    Works Consulted 46
    On the Internet 47
Glossary 47
Index 48

Zeus often relied on the awesome power of his thunderbolts. Sometimes all he had to do was threaten to throw one, and it was sufficient to settle whatever dispute had angered him in the first place.

ZEUS

CHAPTER 1
The Birth of Zeus

Zeus (ZOOS) was the most powerful of all the gods in Greek mythology. He ruled over both gods and mankind from his throne atop Mount Olympus—the highest mountain in Greece.

Even though Zeus was all-powerful, his birth was full of danger. In fact, it was uncertain whether the baby Zeus would even grow up to become the ruler of the universe.

Tricking Cronus

Rhea (REE-uh) was terribly sad and depressed. She was the wife of Cronus (KROH-nus), the ruler of the entire universe. At one time Cronus had been a valiant warrior—one of the mighty Titans who ruled the earth and stars in the early days. While his five older brothers had cowered in fear, Cronus alone had dared to pick up the powerful sickle that his mother, Gaia (GY-uh), also known as Mother Earth, had made from the hardest flint in the world. Then, armed with that awesome weapon, he had confronted his father the Sky, who was called Uranus (YOO-ruh-nus).

Uranus had angered his wife Gaia by rejecting her children, the three one-eyed Cyclopes (sy-KLOH-peez)—Lightning, Thunder, and Vivid, or Thunderbolt—and three other children, who had 50 heads and 100 arms. Uranus had not liked these children, for they were not handsome or beautiful, as a god should be. He had gathered up the six of them and banished them to Tartarus (TAR-tuh-rus). This was a place deep inside the earth, the lowest region of the Underworld, as far below earth as earth is from heaven, with no light and no chance of escape.

CHAPTER 1

As all mothers do, Gaia loved her children, no matter their appearance. She was furious about what Uranus had done—that was why she had made the sickle. It was her plan to give the sickle to her other sons, the Titans—who were taller and stronger than mountains, and beautiful, as gods should be. They would fight Uranus with it and force him to free her other children from Tartarus.

Rhea hands her husband, Cronus, a stone wrapped up so that he will think it is the baby Zeus. Cronus swallows the stone and thinks that he has prevented Zeus from someday replacing him. Rhea spirits the baby away and hides him.

But the Titans shook with fear when their mother asked them to fight their father. They knew that Uranus was very powerful. Only Cronus had had the courage to confront him. When Uranus saw the sickle, he knew that he could not defeat Cronus, so Cronus became the master of the universe.

At first Cronus ruled well. It was a Golden Age. Crimes such as murder and theft were unknown; homes did not need to have locks. Humans and their gods lived in peace and harmony.

One thing that Cronus did not do was free his brothers trapped in Tartarus. This angered Gaia. She knew that someday, a child of Cronus' would be able to defeat him, just as he had defeated his father. So she waited.

Cronus, however, had no intention of being bested by one of his children. Every time his wife, Rhea, had a child, Cronus swallowed it. Safely inside their father, the infants could never grow up and harm him.

THE BIRTH OF ZEUS

This is why Rhea was so sad. All of her sisters had their children around them, playing and keeping them company. Rhea had no one. She was lonely and depressed, knowing that Cronus would continue to swallow her babies.

One day Rhea had an idea. She begged Gaia to help her keep her next child safe from Cronus. Mother Earth smiled. She had been waiting for this moment for years—it was the chance to get back at Cronus. She gladly told Rhea how to trick him.

The next time Rhea was ready to have a child, she went to the island of Crete. There, in a deep cave, she had the baby and gave it to Gaia. When Cronus asked for the child, Rhea wrapped a stone in baby clothes and gave that to him. Cronus was fooled. He swallowed the stone, believing he had once again prevented one of his children from challenging him.

Meanwhile, Gaia took the baby god, who was named Zeus, to either Mount Ida or Mount Dicte. His golden cradle was hung upon a tree so that Cronus would not find him either in heaven or earth, nor in the sea. There, nymphs raised him. To make sure that Cronus would never hear the baby crying, she put armed creatures around the tree and told them to be as noisy as possible. The creatures banged their shields and spears, and this noise drowned out the baby's cries so well that Cronus never found him.

The All-Powerful Zeus
Protected in this way, Zeus grew quickly. He ate and drank ambrosia and nectar, which flowed from the horns of the goat Amaltheia (uh-MAL-thee-uh) and was the food of the gods. Zeus matured into a powerful young god.

Before he left the cave, he thanked the nymphs for raising him by giving them Amaltheia's horns. They were known as horns of plenty, because they never ran out of ambrosia and nectar. He also made a plate from the hide of the goat to cover his body. It was called the Aegis. No arrow or spear could penetrate it.

CHAPTER 1

Now he was almost ready to face Cronus. First, however, he married Metis (MEE-tis), the daughter of one of the Titans. Metis was very smart and had a lot of common sense. She warned Zeus not to fight Cronus alone, because of the power of the other Titans who were with him. She told Zeus that he had to have allies too.

Metis decided to trick Cronus. She gave him a magic herb to eat, which he thought would make him unable to be defeated. In reality, the herb made him sick. He vomited up all five of Rhea's children that he had swallowed. These five children were the deities Hades (HAY-deez), king of the Underworld; Poseidon (poh-SY-dun), god of the sea; Hestia (HES-tee-uh), goddess of the hearth and protector of homes; Demeter (DIH-mih-ter), goddess of agriculture; and Hera (HAYR-uh), queen of heaven. They quickly joined Zeus against Cronus.

When Cronus saw that these six young gods were against him, he knew that he could not beat them. He was driven from the sky and either imprisoned in a region that exists between the earth and sea or placed in an eternal sleep.[1] Zeus became the master of the universe.

The other Titans were angry. They did not want these new gods ruling over them. They decided to fight Zeus and his brothers and sisters.

Zeus had already released the Cyclopes and the others from Tartarus. In gratitude the Cyclopes made lightning bolts, which they gave to Zeus as weapons. They made weapons for the other gods as well. Armed with his thunderbolts, Zeus was unstoppable. No one could defeat him, including the Titans. He subdued them and imprisoned them in Tartarus, "buried by the will of the king of the heavens."[2]

At last, it might have seemed as if Zeus would be able to rule the universe in peace. What he did not realize was that by locking the Titans in Tartarus, he had angered his former friend, Gaia.

THE BIRTH OF ZEUS

Zeus (left) fights the terrible monster Typhon. Although in myth Typhon had numerous heads, ancient art shows it with just one. Typhon was so fearsome that Zeus was initially frightened of it. He recovered his courage and battled it in an epic struggle.

The Battle with Typhon

Gaia sent two monsters, Typhon (TY-fon) and Echidna (eh-KID-nah), to attack Zeus. Typhon was by far the worst. It had 100 heads that touched the stars, and each head's mouth spit lava and boiling hot stones. Venom dripped from its eyes. According to Hesiod:

> Flaming monster with a hundred heads,
> Who rose up against all the gods.
> Death whistled from his fearful jaws,
> His eyes flashed glaring fire.[3]

The creature was so terrifying that at first the gods were frightened—but soon Zeus regained his courage and began to fight Typhon. Seeing Zeus, the other gods came to help him. A terrible battle raged. Typhon tore up entire mountains and hurled them at the gods.

CHAPTER 1

Zeus continued to battle Typhon with his thunderbolts. Then Typhon made a mistake. He tore Mount Aetna from the ground to hurl at the gods just when Zeus hit the mountain with 100 thunderbolts. With a shudder, the mountain fell back and landed right on top of Typhon, trapping him beneath it. The Greeks believed that is where he stayed. Whenever he tried to break free, the mountaintop would fill with fire and smoke.

Echidna fled to a cave with Typhon's terrible children, including the many-headed Hydra. Zeus did not destroy them but let them live, so that heroes would be able to battle them to prove their bravery.

At last, Zeus could rule in peace. The wars had stopped. Gaia did not fight him anymore. Gradually the earth healed from the terrible wars. The mountains stood firm, the rivers were calm, and the earth itself grew green and healthy.

It was the beginning of a time when people could enjoy the earth, under the watchful eye of Zeus. Even so, things could still go wrong.

Analysis

The story of the birth of Zeus was the ancient Greek explanation for the creation of the world. All cultures have creation stories—an attempt for people to understand how the universe and the earth appeared. Although the stories have different elements and characters in them, the basic idea is often the same: how the world was created out of some violent upheaval.

One major difference between the Greek creation stories and some others is that the Greeks have the universe creating the gods—not the other way around. Creation stories in some other cultures have the Supreme Ruler figure appearing first, and then the universe and earth being created next.

The Titans

Gaia (or Gaea) on an ancient coin. She was also known as Mother Earth.

Even before Zeus and the other gods that surrounded him on Mount Olympus, there were the Titans, the first great race of beings. The Titans are sometimes called the elder gods. They ruled the universe for many years. They were incredibly large and enormously strong. The parents of the Titans were Uranus (heaven) and Gaia (earth).

There were twelve Titans all together. The most important of these, besides Cronus, who overthrew his father and became supreme ruler, were Oceanus, a water god; his beautiful wife Tethys (TEH-thus); Mnemosyne (nee-MOH-zee-nee), the goddess of memory; Hyperion (hy-PEER-ee-uhn), the father of the sun, the moon, and the dawn; Iapetus (EYE-uh-PEE-tus), the father of Prometheus (proh-MEE-thee-us), the god who created human beings; and Themis, the goddess of justice. The other Titans were Coeus (KOY-us), Rhea, Phoebe (FEE-bee), Crius (KRY-us), and Theia (THAY-uh).

These Titans gave birth to other Titans. The most notable of these were the four sons of Iapetus. Besides Prometheus, these were Atlas, who with his great strength carried the world on his shoulders; Epimetheus (eh-pih-MEE-thee-us); and Menoetius (mee-noh-EE-shus). Eventually, Zeus and the younger gods rose up and defeated Cronus, and won control of the universe for themselves. Some scholars have noted that the stories of the Titans and the Zeus-led gods are similar to those in other cultures, such as are found in Scandanavia and Babylon. The final results are as different as the stories; sometimes the new gods rise up to defeat the older ones, and sometimes the older ones win. There are even differences in the Greek stories of Zeus and the Titans, depending upon which Greek poet conveyed the myth.

The war between the Mount Olympus gods and the Titans is known as the Titanomachy (The War of the Titans). However, even though Zeus won and sent the Titans to live in exile in Tartarus, some of the Titans who did not fight Zeus, such as Prometheus, survived to join those who governed the universe from Mount Olympus.

Canyon Creek Library

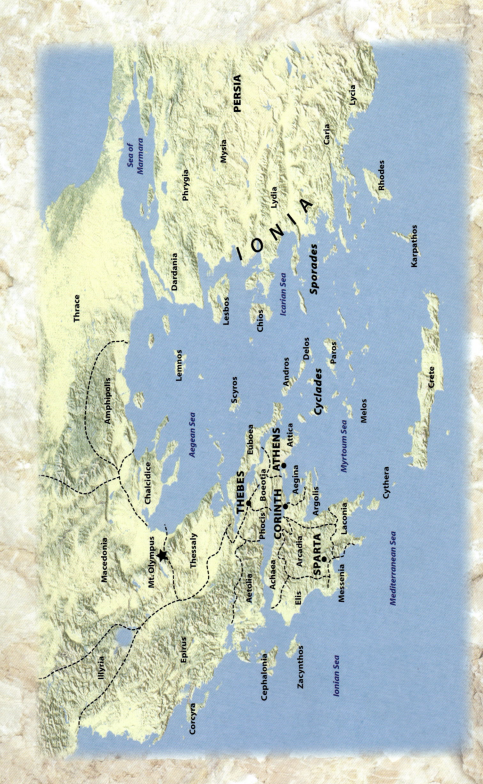

The ancient Greeks believed Zeus and the other gods ruled the universe from atop Mount Olympus in the city-state of Macedonia. There were many Greek city-states. In a time of kingdoms and empires, the Greek city-state—each independent of the others—was a unique idea in government.

CHAPTER 2
The Greek World

The Greece that honored Zeus as the king of all gods was much different from the country of today. Ancient Greece, as it is often called, was settled by the Greeks around 2200 BCE. Its culture blossomed, and poets began recording their myths around 850 BCE. Back then, Greece was not one country. Instead, it was divided into hundreds of small entities called the poleis—city-states. Each city-state (or polis) was independent of the others, meaning that each had its own government. The city-state was a new idea in a world dominated by large countries and sprawling empires such as that of Persia.

The government of the city-state often consisted of a group of individuals. This was another new idea when monarchies were so common. The main idea behind city-state government was to avoid the type of strong, one-person rule that a king or queen enjoyed. Governing power was generally in the hands of citizens—which meant all free men and women, but did not include slaves or people from other countries. (Even though free women were citizens, they did not have equal rights in such matters as voting.) Power was often held by a small and tight-knit group of people, but at least it was not as dictatorial as a king. This type of "people's rule" would have its ultimate expression in Athens, when a man named Cleisthenes would devise an even more radical form of government in which citizens would vote on every issue. This type of "pure democracy" would eventually help Athens become one of the premier city-states in Greece, and a leader in the world.

The city-state usually consisted of a center with public buildings and homes. Outside the center were fields for farming and grazing

CHAPTER 2

The Erechtheion was one of the temples on the acropolis of Athens. Inside were altars to several gods, including Athena, Poseidon, and Zeus.

animals. People also lived in these areas outside the urban center, in villages or on farms.

The city-state also had several other very important areas. One was an open-air public gathering place, where merchants would sell wares and ordinary citizens would gather to shop and converse. Another important area was a wall, usually made of earth or stone, that protected the city. In times of enemy invasion, the people from the surrounding countryside would flee into the city for safety and to fight from behind the walls. Finally, most city-states had an acropolis, which was the highest point in the city, where the temple of the god that protected the city was usually located.

By about 500 BCE, Sparta was the most powerful Greek city-state. It had the mightiest army and had built an empire of other regions and city-states. The Spartans were obsessed with military power. Every action was geared toward having the finest army, and they structured their society accordingly. Any deformed child born that was not likely to be made into a suitable soldier was killed. Young boys began military training around age seven so that by twenty, they were ready to enter the army. Men were then made to live in army barracks for ten years. Military service as a foot soldier was mandatory for all men from the ages of twenty through sixty.

Athens, which was developing a unique all-inclusive form of democracy, was afraid that Sparta would see them as a rival and attack them. They asked for help from King Darius I of the Persian Empire, the strongest empire in the world. When the Spartan threat

THE GREEK WORLD

Alexander the Great from Macedonia was one of the greatest military geniuses of all time. Along with his father Philip, he ended the power of the Greek city-states.

collapsed, the Athenians in 499 BCE tried to help Greeks in Ionia revolt against the same Persian Empire from which they had just sought help. This caused a war with Persia.

It was expected that Persia would defeat the outnumbered Greeks. Instead, on the plains of Marathon in 490 BCE, the Athenians routed the superior Persian forces. According to legend, a Greek messenger ran all the way from Marathon to Athens (about 42 kilometers, or 26 miles) to bring news of the victory. This run is the basis for modern marathon races.

Although Persia would make another attempt to defeat Athens in another war, that too would fail and contribute to the weakening of the Persian Empire. Athens would remain a power among city-states

CHAPTER 2

and in the world until its disastrous Peloponnesian War with Sparta, which lasted from 431 to 404 BCE. That war ended in defeat for Athens.

Remarkably, Athens managed to bounce back from their loss to Sparta and again become a leader among Greek city-states. Four major Greek city-states competed for leadership: Athens, Sparta, Thebes, and Corinth. But the constant rivalry and warfare among these four and their respective allies merely resulted in weakening them all without one emerging victorious. Thus the city-states were ripe to be overthrown by a strong invading power.

That power came from Macedonia to the north, in the person of King Philip II and his son Alexander the Great. The invading Macedonian Army swept forward, and the Greeks were too weak to stop it. In 338 BCE, the Greeks were forced to acknowledge Philip as their leader. This ended the power of the Greek city-states.

This was the political world that the Greeks knew. But what about their gods?

One of the most surprising things about the Greek gods, including Zeus, was that they were all portrayed in the image of people. This was an extraordinary, as well as new, idea. Previously, the images of gods had all been of creatures that were not realistic in any way. Gods were often portrayed as having some combination of human bodies and animal heads, or human heads and animal bodies. The images were somber, serious, and often frightening. An Egyptian god with the head of a fearsome animal was not something that a person would like to meet at night.

The Greek gods were different. They were portrayed in the image of people, and most of the time, the image was pleasant. The men were handsome and the women beautiful. As Edith Hamilton, a celebrated mythology scholar, said: "With the coming forward of Greece, mankind became the center of the universe, the most important thing in it. This was a revolution in thought. Human beings had

THE GREEK WORLD

counted for little heretofore. In Greece man first realized what mankind was."[1]

Greeks who looked around at their world found much to enjoy about it. They made their statues and pictures of the gods to be pleasing, and also pleasantly human. When a Greek artist looked at the strongly muscled bodies of the athletes in the Olympic Games, he set out to duplicate that form in his depictions of the gods. When a sculptor saw a muscular, lean body of a discus thrower, it was only natural that he transfer that image to his statue of Zeus or another god. When he saw a beautiful woman in the marketplace, she became a goddess. As Hamilton again noted: "Greek artists and poets realized how splendid a man could be, straight and swift and strong. He was the fulfillment of their search for beauty. They had no wish to create some fantasy shaped in their own minds. All the art and all the thought of Greece centered in human beings."[2]

The Greek world was one of beauty, and a delightful place to be. "The joy of life is written upon everything the Greeks left behind,"[3] noted Hamilton.

Another thing that was different about the Greek myths was that they were always grounded in reality. For all of the fantastic monsters in the stories and incredible feats that the gods and goddesses performed, they always returned to a real place. Mount Olympus, the home of the gods, is an actual mountain in northern Greece, and is indeed the highest point in the whole country. After one of his incredible adventures, Hercules always returned to his home in the real city of Thebes. Pegasus, the winged horse that traveled through the skies, came back at night to a stable in the actual town of Corinth. This was very different from the myths and stories of the past, in which the gods and beings in the story were mysterious.

The Greek stories attempted to make sense of the world around them in terms that could be explained realistically. Even though Zeus was a fantastic figure, with many powers, he also had his thunder-

CHAPTER 2

bolts, which helped the Greeks understand lightning and thunder. The rising and setting of the sun is explained as Apollo in his chariot driving the sun across the sky. A volcanic eruption is explained in the story of Typhon, who was trapped under the mountain and occasionally struggled to get free.

In the Greek myths can be seen the very early beginnings of modern science, as the people attempted to explain the world around them. As Hamilton points out, magic hardly ever appears in the Greek myths.[4] Magic is unexplainable, and the Greeks wanted explanations. They were not interested in just saying that magic was the reason for an event.

However, not all the stories have a purpose; some are just fun. They are for entertainment, meant for enjoyment and pleasure. If some of the myths show the very early beginnings of science, others contain the seeds of modern entertainment as well. Literature, theatrical plays, movies, television—all can be traced back to the Greeks.

As the Greeks tried to make sense of the world, the character of Zeus changed. In the beginning, it seemed that he was much more concerned with the weather. Scholars have found links to words in the ancient languages of Sanskrit (*dyaus*) and Latin (*dies*, meaning "the day") in the name Zeus.[5] This implies that at first, Zeus was the god of the sky and the weather that it produced, such as wind, lightning, and rain.

Then Zeus began to change. His weather-making abilities were replaced by a sense of justice and fairness toward all mankind. He protected the weak as well as the strong, and he punished the wicked. He loved all his mortal children.

So Zeus ruled humanity from high atop Mount Olympus—but he was not alone. Alongside him were those with whom he shared power—his brothers and sisters, some of his children, and one goddess who had two possible origins.

Cleisthenes

The Parthenon in Athens is a symbol of democracy.

Cleisthenes, a politician, is often credited with putting Athens on the road to government by the people. He has been called the father of democracy.

Cleisthenes was born around 570 BCE. He was a member of the aristocratic Alcmaeonidae (alk-mee-ON-uh-dee) family. Peisistratus (pye-SIS-tret-us), the ruling tyrant of Athens, was overthrown. Both Cleisthenes and Isagoras were rivals for power. Cleisthenes appealed for support to the general population of Athens—something that had never been done before. The aristocratic classes were expected to rule, and the general population was expected to be ruled by them.

Isagoras won by getting help from the Spartans. He forced the Alcmaeonidae family, including Cleisthenes, into exile. But when Isagoras attempted to dissolve the Athens governing council, the citizens revolted. Isagoras and his followers attempted to hang on but were forced to give up after several days. Cleisthenes was recalled from exile and put in charge of Athens. What he then did revolutionized the idea of government. Cleisthenes reorganized the political structure of Athens according to where a citizen lived. He established ten new tribes that were run by people who were chosen based on general selection, rather than by a person's birth or heritage. Thus, anyone could become a leader—a truly unique idea at the time.

The existing ruling council, known as the boule, was increased to 500 members—fifty from each of the ten tribes. Any common citizen in good standing was eligible for membership in the boule—another groundbreaking idea. The members of the boule met and proposed laws for the assembly of voters in Athens. They then voted—one man, one vote—to pass the laws, reject them, or return them for amendments. In this way did the common citizens of Athens have complete control over the laws passed to govern them. No longer was government limited to a select few.

Cleisthenes is believed to have died around 507 BCE.

F.Y.I. — for your info

Zeus speaks to the eagle Aquila on a kylix (a small drinking cup), painted between 510 and 580 BCE. The eagle is the bird most associated with Zeus. Aquila served as Zeus' personal messenger and animal companion. It was given a place among the stars as a constellation.

ZEUS

CHAPTER 3
On Mount Olympus

The gods on Mount Olympus, including Zeus, sat on twelve golden thrones. From there they could rule over heaven and earth. The bird of Zeus was an eagle, and his tree was the mighty oak. Zeus was usually pictured as a mature man, with wavy hair and a curly beard. He wore a long robe that left part of his chest and his right arm free. Very often on his forehead was a crown of oak leaves.

Zeus sat on the tallest throne. Alongside him was a bucket full of thunderbolts. Usually he had only to reach for them to end whatever was bothering him, because the other gods knew about the terrible power that the thunderbolts possessed and stopped whatever they were doing that was angering Zeus.

Zeus would sometimes boast about being the most powerful god. As he told the others: "Let no god, let no goddess attempt to curb [defy] my will . . . you will discover with whom you have to deal."[1]

There was, however, a power that was even greater than Zeus. It was that of Moros, or Destiny. Zeus knew he could not change things that were destined to happen. Even if he'd had the power to do so, he knew it would introduce confusion and uncertainty into the universe. Since he governed the universe, the last thing he wanted was for it to be chaotic.

His oracle (the response by Zeus to a human question, as well as the actual place where the response was given) was centered around a great oak tree at the Greek town of Dodona (doh-DOH-nuh). Priests would interpret the rustling of the leaves of the oak tree, how doves moved when they landed on it, the banging of brass pots that were hung from the branches, and the sound of water gurgling in a nearby fountain as the words of Zeus. It was one of the most respected

CHAPTER 3

oracles of the time, and was consulted by Greeks and foreigners alike.

Sitting with Zeus on Mount Olympus were the following:

Hera, his sister and wife, and therefore the queen of heaven, sat to his right. She was incredibly jealous, and always sought revenge against the many women—both mortal and immortal—with whom Zeus had relationships. She was the goddess of marriage and the protector of women.

Next to Hera sat her son Ares (AIR-eez), the god of war. Despite the frequent wars in Greek history, Ares does not play a major role in Greek mythology.

Sitting next to Ares was the beautiful and mysterious Aphrodite (af-roh-DY-tee), the goddess of love and beauty. Although she sometimes is credited as the daughter of Zeus, she is also supposed to have sprung from the foam of the ocean waves.

Next in line was Hephaestus (huh-FES-tuhs), the god of fire. He was portrayed as ugly and lame (he could not walk well), the only god among the beautiful and handsome Olympians to be so described, yet kind and peaceful. He constructed the buildings on Mount Olympus and the weapons for the gods.

Alongside Hephaestus was Hermes (HUR-meez), Zeus's son, as well as his messenger. Wings on his sandals and hat let him move with the speed of the wind.

On the end was Zeus' sister Demeter. As the goddess of the harvest, the Greeks often called upon her to bless their crops. Always with Demeter was her daughter Persephone (pur-SEF-uh-nee), whose story explains the seasons.

On Zeus' left sat Poseidon, lord of the sea. In his hand he held a powerful trident. When he struck the ground with it, the earth quaked. In the water, it caused great waves and howling winds. One of his favorite things to do was ride the waves in a chariot pulled by a team of snow-white horses. He had almost as many love affairs as Zeus.

ON MOUNT OLYMPUS

The Temple of Olympian Zeus in Athens. Construction on the temple began in 515 BCE, but it was not finished until 129 CE—well after the Romans had conquered Greece. The Romans dedicated the temple to Jupiter, their name for Zeus. Only 15 of the original 104 columns still stand. Each is about 56 feet (17 meters) tall.

Next to Poseidon was Athena (uh-THEE-nuh), daughter of Zeus. She was the goddess of wisdom and reason, as well as of civilized life. She sprang, fully grown, from Zeus's head. In earlier Greek tales she is also a fierce fighter. It was she who invented the bridle so that people could tame horses. Zeus liked her so much that he trusted her to carry his breastplate, the Aegis, and also his thunderbolts.

Next on Zeus' left were the male and female twins Apollo (ah-PAH-loh) and Artemis (AR-teh-mis). Apollo was the god of prophecy (he could predict the future), light, and music. He entertained the gods on Mount Olympus by playing tunes on his golden lyre. As

CHAPTER 3

the god of light, he never told a lie. He was also the first to show humanity how to heal (from sickness, injuries, etc.), and so he was known as the god of healing. Artemis, the goddess of the hunt, was also known as the Lady of Wild Things. Wild animals were sacred to her, especially deer. She was often portrayed with a bow and quiver (holder for arrows), and dogs.

Finally, in the last seat was gentle Dionysus (dy-oh-NY-sus). Youngest of the Olympians, he was the god of the vine (as in grapes, for making wine). He was the only god on Mount Olympus who was the son of a mortal woman.

These were the eleven gods who sat along either side of Zeus on Mount Olympus. Two other gods who helped Zeus rule were Hestia, the goddess of the hearth, and Hades, lord of the Underworld.

Hestia did not have a throne, but took care of the sacred fire on Mount Olympus. She was the gentlest of all the gods. As the hearth goddess she was also the symbol of the fires that burned in every human home for cooking and light, and she watched over every home. As such, mortal meals began and ended with an offering to her. She otherwise plays no major role in the stories in Greek mythology.

Silent and gloomy, Hades did not stay on Mount Olympus with the other gods. Instead he remained underground, in his mysterious palace, from where he ruled over the land of the dead.

These were the immortals who helped Zeus govern the universe. The twelve gods who sat with Zeus on Mount Olympus ate nectar and ambrosia, just as Zeus had when he was growing up. The gods could not die. In their veins was ichor instead of blood, and this substance made them invincible. Even when they were wounded, their bodies quickly healed. The gods also could change themselves into animals or inanimate objects if they wished,[2]—and Zeus was a master of disguises.

Demeter, Persephone, and Hades

The god of the Underworld, Hades, grabs Persephone.

One of the deities who inhabited Mount Olympus with Zeus was Demeter, the goddess of the harvest. Always with Demeter was her beautiful daughter, Persephone. The two of them were involved in one of Zeus' most important decisions . . . one that would explain the changing seasons in the Greek world.

Persephone was so lovely and so beautiful that when she danced on the earth while Demeter looked after her green trees and fields of lush crops, flowers would pop up behind her every step. Persephone's beauty and grace attracted the attention of Hades, lord of the Underworld. He did not live on Mount Olympus, but underground, in his gloomy, cold kingdom of death. Hades was so taken with Persephone that he decided he must have her for his wife.

One day, while Demeter was on earth, Persephone wandered away from her. This was the chance Hades had been waiting for. The ground split open in front of the girl and out came a dark chariot drawn by black horses. Hades grabbed Persephone and carried her down to his underground kingdom.

When Demeter realized her daughter was gone, she frantically raced all about but could not find her. Meanwhile, Hades was giving Persephone beautiful clothes and brilliant jewels, but nothing made her happy. She did not want this dark, cold place—she wanted the warmth of the sun, the flowers, and her mother.

All Demeter could think about was her missing daughter. The world grew cold and hard because she neglected it. Nothing could grow while she cried and looked for her daughter. People and animals starved. Zeus, who could not let the world die, ordered Hades to release Persephone. However, the girl had eaten some forbidden fruit while in the Underworld, so she could not totally escape.

Zeus ruled that Persephone had to spend part of the year with Hades and part with Demeter. When she and her mother are together, the world is warm and green (spring and summer). When they are apart and Persephone is with Hades, the world turns cold and lifeless (fall and winter).

F.Y.I. for your info

Zeus and Hera (left) were husband and wife. However, that did not stop Zeus from becoming romantically involved with other women, which distressed the extremely jealous Hera.

ZEUS

CHAPTER 4

The Amorous Adventures of Zeus

Many of the legends and stories about Zeus have to do with the many women with whom he had a romance. Zeus was constantly attracted to pretty women, goddesses and mortals alike. He would use whatever methods he could to get a woman to love him—even deception. Typical of his actions was the story of how he convinced the goddess Hera to marry him.

Although very beautiful, Hera was also very jealous. She was one of the twelve gods who sat on thrones on Mount Olympus, and she saw firsthand how Zeus was when it came to women. When Zeus asked her to be his wife, Hera refused.

Zeus was not so easily denied. He created a mighty thunderstorm, then changed himself into a small cuckoo bird that was apparently having trouble flying in the weather (some sources say the bird was cold in winter[1]). Seeking shelter, the bird flew into Hera's arms for safety. Hera felt sorry for the small, wet bird and hugged it close to her to keep it warm. The bird vanished, and in its place Hera was holding Zeus. She soon married him.

The wedding of Zeus and Hera was a joyous occasion. All nature burst forth in bloom of celebration. Gaia gave Hera an apple tree whose golden apples would grant immortality. Hera loved the tree. She planted it in the secret garden of the Hesperides (hes-PAIR-ih-deez), a group of nymphs. A dragon with 100 heads guarded the tree, and the Hesperides cared for it.

The warm glow of Zeus and Hera's marriage did not last. Zeus was attracted to many pretty girls, and when Hera found out about these other relationships, she got very angry. She and Zeus argued constantly. Hera would take her anger out on the women with whom

CHAPTER 4

Zeus had relationships, even though she knew from personal experience how Zeus could deceive others.

Zeus and Io

Zeus' deceitful nature and Hera's anger are both evident in the story of Io (EYE-oh). One day Hera looked down on earth and saw a thundercloud where no cloud should have been. (In an alternate version of the story, Zeus wrapped the earth in a dark cloud that obscured the daylight.) Suspecting it was Zeus in disguise, she rushed down to Earth and ordered the cloud away. Standing there was Zeus, all right, and next to him was a fluffy white cow.

Zeus had been with a beautiful girl named Io, but when he realized that Hera was coming, he had quickly changed Io into a cow to protect her. Hera was not fooled. Guessing what Zeus was up to, she asked him for the pretty animal as a present.

Zeus was trapped. He had to give Hera the cow. Hera tied Io to a tree, and told her servant Argus to watch over it. Argus was the ideal watchman, because he had 100 eyes placed all over his body. He never closed more than half of them at one time.

Zeus came to Io as a cloud.

Poor Io raised her eyes to Mount Olympus for help, but Zeus was so afraid of what Hera would do if she found out the truth, he dared not come to the girl's aid. At last he asked clever Hermes, the messenger of the gods, to help him. Hermes went to earth, where he disguised himself as a shepherd. Then he approached Argus, playing his pipe and telling a long, boring story. Finally Argus fell asleep. Hermes then either killed Argus or made him sleep forever; then he set Io free.

The Amorous Adventures of Zeus

Hera found a way to honor Argus by putting his eyes on the tail of the peacock. She continued to torment Io, but she eventually let Zeus change her back to human form, as long as he would have nothing to do with her.

Zeus and Semele

Sometimes Hera's jealousy could make her act incredibly cruel. That is what happened when Zeus fell in love with the mortal girl Semele (SEH-muh-lee). Hera found out about the relationship and vowed revenge. She disguised herself as a mortal and convinced Semele to ask Zeus to come to her in all his godlike magnificence. When Semele asked him to do this, Zeus desperately begged her to change her mind, but the girl insisted.

Finally Zeus gave in and granted Semele her wish. The sight of him in his chariot, surrounded by lightning and thunder, was too much for mortal eyes to see—just as Hera knew it would be. Semele, who was pregnant with Zeus' child, was consumed by fire.

Zeus took pity on the unborn baby inside Semele, rescued it, and brought it to Mount Olympus, where he enclosed it in his own thigh until it was ready to be born. The baby became Dionysus, the god of wine.

The Many Shapes of Zeus

To trick women into having affairs with him, Zeus would often take on a disguise. One day a beautiful girl named Europa (yur-OH-puh) was gathering flowers at the water's edge. Nearby was a herd of bulls. One bull in particular caught Europa's attention. He was very regal-looking, with an attractive coat of hair, but at the same time very peaceful. The girl approached the animal, who knelt down before her. Europa climbed onto the gentle bull's back and began putting garlands of flowers around the animal's horns.

What Europa did not know was that the animal was Zeus. He had changed into this shape to trick the girl because he had

CHAPTER 4

In the story of Zeus and Europa, Zeus changes himself into a bull to fool the girl.

fallen in love with her. With Europa firmly on his back, he jumped to his feet and raced across the water until they reached the southern coast of Crete (an island off the southeast coast of Greece). There, under a shady tree, Zeus made the girl his mistress. The tree was allowed to keep its leaves all year long because it had witnessed the divine union.

Another time, Zeus wanted to make love to a married woman named Leda (LEE-duh). One evening, while bathing in a pool of water, Leda saw a magnificent white swan coming toward her. It was Zeus, who then made love with the woman.

On another occasion, Zeus wanted to have a son who would protect gods and man alike, and he knew that a married woman named Alcmene should be the mother. Zeus waited until her husband, Amphitryon, was away, and then took on the man's form. When Alcmene saw that her "husband" had come home, she was very happy and spent time with him. (When the real Amphitryon later returned, he was puzzled by his wife's apparent disinterest in him, even though he had been gone awhile.) From Alcmene's union with Zeus was born the mighty Hercules (HER-kyoo-leez), one of the greatest champions of all time, who did indeed protect both gods and man.

In another story, a man named Acrisius had a daughter named Danae. When an oracle told Acrisius that his daughter would have a child who would cause his death, he panicked and locked the woman and her nurse into an underground chamber. This hardly

The Amorous Adventures of Zeus

stopped Zeus, who had fallen in love with Danae. He turned himself into a shower of gold and so was able to get into the chamber and see Danae. From his relationship with Danae was born a son named Perseus (PER-see-us). After some adventures, he did indeed accidentally cause Acrisius' death.

Hera's Revenge . . . Maybe

Even gods can get on each other's nerves, and so it was with Zeus. His numerous liaisons with other women bothered Hera, and his constant pride in his power annoyed the other gods. They decided to get revenge.

One day, all the gods except Hestia crept up to where Zeus was sleeping on his couch. They tied him to the couch with strong rawhide strips, and knotted them into 100 knots, so that not even Zeus could untie them. They moved his bucket of thunderbolts safely out of reach, then stepped back.

Oh, how Zeus yelled when he awoke and saw that he was securely tied. He threatened them with death and all types of other terrible things. The other gods just laughed.

However, as the other gods were talking about who was going to succeed him as king of the gods, a sea-nymph named Thetis went off to find the Titan Briareus, who had 100 hands. Thetis feared that with Zeus gone, there would be a civil war on Mount Olympus. Briareus used all his hands at once to untie the knots and free Zeus. The gods' rebellion had failed.

Zeus took revenge on Hera by hanging her up in the sky with a golden bracelet around each wrist and an anvil tied to each ankle. Eventually he freed her when the other gods all promised not to rebel against him again.

Hera apparently learned her lesson, telling the other gods how it was useless to try to defeat Zeus. "How foolish we are to become angry with Zeus. . . . He sits apart, for he boasts of being incontestably superior to the immortal gods in might. So resign yourselves."[2]

CHAPTER 4

Sometimes women tried to run away rather than be with Zeus. However, the king of the gods was always quicker.

Possible Meanings

These are just some of the many stories about Zeus and his desire for female companionship. But are they just stories, or do they have deeper meanings?

Just as the story of Zeus' birth and fight with Cronus is an attempt to explain the creation of the world, it seems likely that some of these stories are explanations of actual events. That Zeus had so many children possibly reflects the desire of many Greek tribes or cities to say that they or the town had a divine beginning. The story of Zeus and Europa may be tied to Crete's worship of a bull god as a religious symbol. When Zeus becomes a shower of gold, it may well represent how golden rays of sunshine penetrate deep into the earth, warming it and causing buried seeds to sprout and grow.

Another possible explanation is that Zeus is a combination of many gods. As the worship of Zeus spread to each Greek town, the existing god was merged into the character of Zeus. Not knowing what to do with the wife of the existing god, she was transferred to Zeus, and became one of the many women with whom he had a relationship.[3]

The Zeus who chased women like a lovesick schoolboy is featured much more in earlier stories about him. As the legends evolved, so did his character. He stopped being a chaser of women and became a symbol of right and justice.

Hercules

Hercules. The name echoes across the centuries as a symbol of strength. Even today, thousands of years after he is supposed to have lived, there are few people who do not know his name.

Hercules, or, as the Greeks called him, Heracles (*Hercules* is the Roman name), was the son of Zeus and Alcmene. Hera, jealous as usual of any evidence of her husband's infidelity, tried to kill the baby Hercules by sending two giant snakes to destroy him. Even at this young age, Hercules proved that he was no ordinary child by strangling them. Later she put a spell on him to make him temporarily insane. This caused him to kill his wife and children. When he recovered his sanity, Hercules wanted to kill himself because of what he had done, but he was advised instead by an oracle to seek forgiveness by serving his cousin Eurystheus. He urged Hercules to complete twelve difficult, if not impossible, tasks—the legendary Twelve Labors of Hercules. In one of the labors, he killed a lion and took its impenetrable skin as a trophy. He is usually shown wearing this skin.

The mighty Hercules constantly used his great strength to battle evil creatures, including the Lernaean Hydra.

Even today, when a job is extremely difficult, it might be referred to as a "labor of Hercules." The tasks Hercules had to perform were difficult indeed. Among them were killing the Hydra, a multiple-headed beast; capturing a deer that was sacred to Artemis, the goddess of the hunt; and obtaining Hera's golden apples from the garden of the Hesperides (meanwhile tricking Atlas into taking back the world after Hercules had held it up for a while).

After his accidental death at the hands of his wife, who thought a vial of poison was a love potion, Hercules was brought to Mount Olympus, where he lived among the gods for the rest of his days. Even to them Hercules was a hero.

Prometheus gave the gift of fire to humanity against the wishes of Zeus. For doing so, Zeus punished him by chaining him to a rock and having an eagle eat his liver every day.

ZEUS

CHAPTER 5
Major Zeus Myths

As the most powerful god, Zeus appears in many stories in which he makes decisions or takes actions that affect the outcome of the story. Many of these, again, are attempts to explain some type of natural occurrence, although some are used to illustrate other characteristics of Zeus. In some stories, such as those below, he figures as the main character.

How Zeus Obtained Wisdom
The first wife of Zeus was Metis. She was smart, and the goddess of prudence. Gaia predicted that if Metis would have a son, he would replace Zeus, just as Zeus had replaced Cronus and Cronus had replaced Uranus.

Zeus was in a predicament. He did not want to lose the sensible advice that Metis gave him, nor did he want her to have a son who would replace him. He resorted to an old Cronus trick and swallowed her when she changed into a fly. Metis went to his head, where she remained ever after, giving Zeus his wise advice.

The Gift of Fire
Zeus told the Titan Prometheus and his brother Epimetheus to put living things on earth. Prometheus carefully made people out of clay. Working more quickly, Epimetheus made many different types of animals and gave them abilities that were superior to those of people. They could see farther, smell better, and run faster than mankind.

Feeling sorry for humanity, Prometheus asked Zeus if he could give them fire. Zeus refused, saying that fire was only for the gods. Prometheus stole fire anyway and gave it to humanity.

CHAPTER 5

Furious at being disobeyed, Zeus decided to punish Prometheus. He bound him to a rock with unbreakable chains. Every day, an eagle came and ate his liver. Every night it grew back, so that the eagle could eat it again the next day. For humanity, Zeus had another punishment in mind. He sent a beautiful woman to earth named Pandora (pan-DOR-uh). Zeus gave her a sealed jar and told her never to open it, but her incredible curiosity made her open it anyway. Out came numerous miseries to plague people, such as greed, envy, lies, gossip, and old age. But Zeus wasn't totally heartless. He also put hope in the jar, and when it was released it also spread through people.

The miseries unleashed by Pandora made the people cruel and cold-hearted. They robbed, stole, and murdered one another. They got so bad that Zeus decided it was necessary to destroy them all and start fresh.

The Journey to Phrygia

There are two great flood stories associated with Zeus. In one, it is said, he would disguise himself and visit the earth in order to observe humanity. He wanted to know whether people were faithfully worshiping the gods, and if a sense of kindness and goodwill existed among humanity.

One day Zeus decided to go to the country of Phrygia (part of modern-day Turkey) and see what things were like there. With him he took his fleet son Hermes, messenger of the gods. Disguised as human travelers, the two walked through Phrygia until they came to a city of fine houses. Zeus knocked at the first house. When the door was opened, he explained that he and Hermes were two tired and hungry travelers. They needed rest and food. The door was slammed in his face. So too were the other doors of the well-to-do houses.

Seething with anger, the two gods came upon a small cabin not nearly as nice as the other homes. When Zeus knocked and requested food and shelter, the old woman who answered the door graciously

MAJOR ZEUS MYTHS

led the two gods inside. "We are poor folk," she said, "but poverty isn't so bad when you're willing to own up to it, and a contented spirit is a great help, too."[1]

For the next few hours the old woman, Baucis, and her elderly husband, Philemon, gladly shared all that they had with the strangers, even though it was not much. They gave them cabbage, bacon, radishes, and cheese to eat, and wine to drink. Eventually the two mortals realized that the amount of wine remaining was always the same, even though much wine had already been consumed. That's when they knew they were in the presence of gods, and pleaded with them to forgive the meagerness of their feast.

Zeus, pleased that he had at last found two people willing to share out of the goodness of their heart, led them outside to the top of a mountain. When Baucis and Philemon looked back, they saw the whole city disappearing under a giant lake—Zeus' punishment for being so uncaring.

The old couple's hut was turned into a magnificent temple of the gods. Baucis and Philemon became the priests of the temple. Because they had asked Zeus to never see the other's grave, when it was their time to die, Zeus turned them into two mighty trees growing from a single trunk.

The Great Flood, Another Version
For some time, Zeus had been aware that humanity had been growing crueler and more vicious by the day. Wars and murders were constant occurrences. People had stopped honoring the gods.

Wanting to see for himself how bad things had become, Zeus journeyed to earth, where he disguised himself as a traveler and went to a castle where a party was under way. Upon arriving, he announced himself as a god and asked for the respect that gods, as well as strangers traveling, should receive. The owner of the house, Lycaon, laughed at him and said that if he wanted to stay the night, in the morning it would be obvious whether or not he was a god.

CHAPTER 5

Zeus knew that Lycaon meant to try to kill him overnight, to prove his immortality. When Lycaon killed another man right in front of Zeus, the great god knew that people had become wicked and cruel beyond any hope of saving. With a snarl Zeus punched the air with his fist, causing a great flash of lightning in the castle.

Finally Lycaon knew that this was a god, and he ran away. But he could not escape Zeus's vengeance. Zeus turned him into a wolf.

As for the rest of humanity, Zeus decided to wipe everyone out and start all over again. At first he thought he would send a great fire to cleanse the earth, but then he realized that the fire might even hurt the mountain where the gods lived. He decided instead to send a great flood.

Deucalion and Pyrrha, painted by Giovanni Benedetto Castiglione around 1665. After Zeus sent the Great Flood, Deucalion and Pyrrha, the only survivors, repopulated the world by throwing stones over their shoulder. The stones turned into people.

MAJOR ZEUS MYTHS

With the help of Aeolus, the keeper of the winds, and Poseidon, Zeus sent down rain and wind to earth, and sent the rivers over the banks and caused the ocean to rise

Then Zeus looked at the peak of a very high mountain and saw two people who had climbed there, Deucalion (doo-KAH-lee-on) and his wife, Pyrrha. (In another version of the story, they are in a boat.) Zeus remembered that they were good people who had honored the gods. He decided to spare their lives and called off the flood. The rain stopped, the ocean and rivers calmed, and the sun came out and began to dry the earth. The only people left were Deucalion and Pyrrha.

Climbing down from the mountain, the two went into a ruined temple of the god Themis. They gave thanks for having their lives spared, but also asked what they should do now that they were the last two people on earth.

"Veil your heads and cast behind you the bones of your mother,"[2] said a voice.

Pyrrha was horrified by the command. "We dare not do such a thing,"[3] she said.

Then Deucalion realized that what the command really meant was that the earth was their mother, and her bones were the stones on the ground. They began walking and throwing stones behind them. As the stones fell, they turned into a new race of people: Deucalion's stones turned into men, and Pyrrha's into women.

This was how Zeus put a new race of people onto the earth, one whose spirit and determination were as hard as stone.

The Island of Delos

Sometimes Poseidon created islands, and one of them was Delos. The island was so new that it was not connected to the earth in any fashion. Only a single palm tree grew on it.

Zeus had fallen in love with the goddess Leto (LEE-toh) and married her. When Hera found out, she was furious, and when it was

CHAPTER 5

A tree on the island of Delos. Zeus rewarded the floating island for giving shelter to Leto by fastening it to the earth.

revealed that Leto was due to give birth to twins, she got even angrier. She ordered all the land on earth to refuse to give Leto shelter. She also forbade Eileithyia (eyl-EYTH-ee-EYE-uh), goddess of childbirth, to help the girl. Leto wandered all over the world, looking for a place to give birth.

Finally she came to Delos. Since it was floating and not attached to any land, it did not have to obey Hera's command. Gratefully Leto rested under the shade of its palm tree. But without Eileithyia, Leto still could not give birth to her babies.

The other gods felt sorry for Leto. They offered Hera a beautiful necklace if she would change her mind. Hera could not resist the necklace, so she let Eileithyia go to Leto. The first baby born was Artemis, goddess of the hunt. The next child was Apollo, god of music, light, and reason.

Zeus was so happy when he saw his beautiful twins that he connected Delos to the earth, right at the spot where it is today—in the Aegean Sea. He took the twins up to sit with him on Mount Olympus. The island of Delos became famous as the birthplace of these two gods, and many people visited the island to worship.

MAJOR ZEUS MYTHS

Zeus Endures

These are some of the better-known stories involving Zeus. As the lord of the universe and the leader of the gods, he is in many others, but often it is just for a brief appearance.

Some of the stories try to explain important things that happened, such as how people first obtained fire. This was a momentous event in the history of humanity, because fire enabled humans to cook their food, light the darkness, and keep the cold away. The story of the flood tries to explain a natural occurrence that probably happened in the distant past. Other cultures also contain stories of great floods. Some Zeus myths are more for entertainment, to fill out the character of Zeus, such as the story of how he obtained wisdom.

Myths have enduring legacies in the modern world. Some writers have used the Greek myths as models for their own work. One such example is Mary Wollstonecraft Shelley, who wrote the novel *Frankenstein*. She subtitled the book "The Modern Prometheus." Images and concepts that appeared in Greek myths are also still with us. For example, when someone does something they should not, and unpleasant consequences result, they've "opened a Pandora's box." As far as Zeus himself, there are companies called Zeus, products called Zeus, and a whole lot more. Constellations are named for mythological characters from his stories, such as Gemini (the twin sons of Zeus) and Aquila, his eagle.

The original Greek myths may have been born deep in the past, but references to them are all around us. It might have surprised the ancient Greeks that the tales they spun of gods and goddesses and their fantastic feats would still exist in some form many thousands of years later . . . but maybe not. After all, the stories of Zeus and the other gods are primarily ways to attempt to explain the world, and people have never stopped trying to do that, whether it was 4,000 years ago or today.

for your info

F.Y.I.

Mary Wollstonecraft Shelley

Mary Wollstonecraft Shelley, a twenty-year-old writer acting on a challenge from a much more famous author, wrote one of the most famous novels in history—*Frankenstein*—and subtitled it with a reference to Greek mythology: *The Modern Prometheus*.

The summer of 1816 was cold and snowy because of the eruption of the volcano Tambora, which changed global weather patterns. Mary Wollstonecraft Goodwin and her soon-to-be husband, the poet Percy Shelley, visited the writer Lord Byron at his vacation villa at Lake Geneva in Switzerland. Because the terrible weather ruined their outdoor plans, Byron proposed that they all try to outdo each other by writing a scary story. Mary's became the novel *Frankenstein,* which was published on January 1, 1818, in London. Although the book was not a critical success, it was very popular among the reading public.

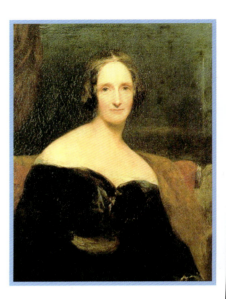

Mary Wollstonecraft Shelley, the writer of the classic novel *Frankenstein*.

On the surface, the connection to Prometheus is obvious. Prometheus is the Greek god who created man and was punished by Zeus. In Shelley's novel, Victor Frankenstein creates a man and is ultimately punished for his action.

On another level, the connection of "The Modern Prometheus" goes deeper. Mary Shelley considered Prometheus bad, not good, for bringing fire to humanity; fire got mankind to eat meat because it could then be cooked, so the gift of fire encouraged people to kill and cook animals, something that angered her. By creating life, Victor Frankenstein, like Prometheus, is a villain who has done a terrible wrong that will echo throughout the centuries.

None of Mary Shelley's other published writings ever approached the popularity of *Frankenstein*. She died in 1851.

Chapter Notes

Chapter 1. The Birth of Zeus

1. Paul Hamlyn, *Greek Mythology* (London, England: Batchworth Press Limited, 1963), p. 15.

2. Ibid.

3. Hesiod, as quoted in Edith Hamilton, *Mythology* (New York: New American Library, 1989), p. 67.

Chapter 2. The Greek World

1. Edith Hamilton, *Mythology* (New York: New American Library, 1989), p. 16.

2. Ibid.

3. Edith Hamilton, *The Greek Way* (New York: W.W. Norton & Company, Inc., 1930), p. 32.

4. Hamilton, *Mythology*, p. 17.

5. Paul Hamlyn, *Greek Mythology* (London, England: Batchworth Press Limited, 1963), p. 23.

Chapter 3. On Mount Olympus

1. Paul Hamlyn, (London, England: Batchworth Press Limited, 1963), p. 22.

2. Ibid.

Chapter 4. The Amorous Adventures of Zeus

1. Paul Hamlyn, *Greek Mythology* (London, England: Batchworth Press Limited, 1963), p. 24.

2. Ibid., p. 22.

3. Edith Hamilton, Mythology (New York: New American Library, 1989), p. 27.

Chapter 5. Major Zeus Myths

1. Edith Hamilton, *Mythology* (New York: New American Library, 1989), p. 112.

2. Ibid., p. 74.

3. Ibid.

FURTHER READING

Books

Burleigh, Robert. *Pandora*. San Diego: Silver Whistle, 2002.

Evslin, Bernard. *Heroes, Gods and Monsters of the Greek Myths*. New York: Dell Laurel-Leaf, 2005.

Osborne, Mary Pope. *The Land of the Dead*. New York: Hyperion Books for Children, 2002.

Spies, Karen Bornemann. *The Iliad and the Odyssey in Greek Mythology*. Berkeley Heights, NJ: Enslow, 2002.

Steig, Jeanne. *A Gift from Zeus: Sixteen Favorite Myths*. New York: Joanna Cotler Books, 2001.

Vinge, Joan D. *The Random House Book of Greek Myths*. New York: Random House, 1999.

Works Consulted

Cartledge, Paul. *The Greeks—Crucible of Civilization*. New York: TV Books, L.L.C., 2000.

Freeman, Charles. *Egypt, Greece and Rome—Civilizations of the Ancient Mediterranean*. New York: Oxford University Press, Inc., 1996.

Graves, Robert. *The Greek Myths*. London, England: Penguin Books, 1992.

Hamilton, Edith. *The Greek Way*. New York: W.W. Norton & Company, 1930.

———. *Mythology*. New York: New American Library, 1989.

Hamlyn, Paul. *Greek Mythology*. London, England: Batchworth Press Limited, 1963.

Johnston, Alan. *The Emergence of Greece*. New York: E.P. Dutton & Co., Inc., 1976.

Kravitz, David. *Who's Who In Greek and Roman Mythology*. New York: Clarkson N. Potter, Inc., 1975.

Martin, Thomas R. *Ancient Greece—From Prehistoric to Hellenistic Times*. New Haven, Connecticut: Yale University Press, 1996.

Moncrieff, A.R. Hope. *A Treasury of Classical Mythology*. New York: Barnes & Noble Books, 1992.

FURTHER READING

On the Internet
Greek Mythology
   http://www.mythweb.com/
The Immortals: Greek Mythology
   http://messagenet.com/myths/chart.html
Encyclopedia Mythica: Greek Mythology
   http://www.pantheon.org/areas/mythology/europe/greek/
Women in Greek Myths
   http://www.paleothea.com/

GLOSSARY

aegis (EE-jis)—The shield of Zeus and Athena, worn over the chest.

ambrosia (am-BROH-jhuh)—The food of the gods, which was reportedly delicious.

amorous (AA-muh-rus)—Having to do with love.

chaos (KAY-os)—Disorder; utter confusion.

deity (DEE-ih-tee)—A god or goddess.

liaison (LEE-uh-zon)—A connection.

lyre (LY-ur)—A handheld, stringed musical instrument much like a harp.

monarchy (MAH-nar-kee)—A government led by a king, queen, or similar ruler.

nectar (NEK-ter)—The drink of the gods, which was reportedly delicious.

nymph (NIMF)—A beautiful young female and lesser nature god that lived in the sea, forest, or other part of the wilderness.

seduce (suh-DOOS)—To corrupt, or to convince someone to have a physical relationship.

somber (SOM-bur)—Gloomy and dark.

INDEX

Acrisius 32, 33
Aeolus 41
Alcmene 32, 33, 35
Alexander the Great 17, 18
Amaltheia 9
Amphitryon 32
Aphrodite 24
Apollo 19, 25, 42
Aquila (eagle) 22, 23, 36, 43
Ares 24
Argus 30
Artemis 25, 35, 42
Athena 21, 25
Baucis 38, 39
Briareus 33
city-states 14, 15–16, 18
Cleisthenes 15, 21
Creation stories 12, 13
Crete 9, 31, 34
Cronus 7–9, 10, 13, 34, 37
Cyclopes 7, 10
Danae 32–33
Darius I 16
Delos 41, 42
Demeter 10, 24, 27
Deucalion 40–41
Dionysus 26, 31
Echidna 11–12
Eileithyia 41, 42
Epimetheus 13, 37
Europa 31–32, 34
Gaia (Gaea) 7, 8, 9, 10, 11–12, 13, 29, 37
Hades 10, 26, 27
Hephaestus 24, 29
Hera 10, 24, 28, 29–31, 33, 35, 41, 42
Hercules (Heracles) 19, 32, 35
Hermes 24, 30, 38–39
Hestia 10, 26, 33
Hydra 12, 35
Io 30

Lycaon 39, 40
Leda 32, 39
Leto 41–42
Metis 10, 37
Moros 23
Mount Aetna 12
Mount Dicte (Mount Ida) 9
Mount Olympus 7, 13, 14, 19, 20, 22, 23, 25, 26, 31, 33, 35, 42
Pandora 38, 43
Pegasus 19
Peloponnesian War 17
Perseus 33
Persephone 24, 27
Persian Empire 16, 17
Philemon 39
Poseidon 10, 20, 24–25, 40–41
Prometheus 13, 36, 37–38, 43, 44
Pyrrha 40–41
Rhea 7–10
Semele 31
Shelley, Mary Wollstonecraft 43, 44
Sparta 16, 17, 21
Tartarus 7, 8, 10
Themis 41
Thetis 33
Titans 7, 8, 10, 13, 33, 37
Typhon 11–12, 20
Uranus 7, 8, 13, 37
Zeus
    aegis of 9
    attributes of 19, 20, 23, 29, 30, 31, 33, 34
    battles Cronus 9–10
    birth of 7, 8, 9, 12
    and flood stories 38–41, 43
    oracle of 23–24
    origins of myth 20
    and romance 28, 29–34, 35
    temple of 25
    thunderbolts 6, 10, 12, 19, 23, 25, 33